Meet the
Dinosaurs

FIRST EDITION
Series Editor Penny Smith; **Art Editor** Leah Germann; **US Editors** Elizabeth Hester, John Searcy;
DTP Designer Almudena Díaz; **Pre-Production Producer** Nadine King; **Producer** Sara Hu;
Picture Research Myriam Megharbi; **Dinosaur Consultant** Dougal Dixon;
Reading Consultant Linda Gambrell, PhD

THIS EDITION
Editorial Management by Oriel Square
Produced for DK by WonderLab Group LLC
Jennifer Emmett, Erica Green, Kate Hale, *Founders*

Editors Grace Hill Smith, Libby Romero, Michaela Weglinski;
Photography Editors Kelley Miller, Annette Kiesow, Nicole DiMella;
Managing Editor Rachel Houghton; **Designers** Project Design Company;
Researcher Michelle Harris; **Copy Editor** Lori Merritt; **Indexer** Connie Binder; **Proofreader** Larry Shea;
Reading Specialist Dr. Jennifer Albro; **Curriculum Specialist** Elaine Larson

Published in the United States by DK Publishing
1745 Broadway, 20th Floor, New York, NY 10019

Copyright © 2023 Dorling Kindersley Limited
DK, a Division of Penguin Random House LLC
22 23 24 25 26 10 9 8 7 6 5 4 3 2 1
001–333367–Mar/2023

A catalog record for this book
is available from the Library of Congress.
HC ISBN: 978-0-7440-6564-0
PB ISBN: 978-0-7440-6565-7

DK books are available at special discounts when purchased
in bulk for sales promotions, premiums, fundraising, or
educational use. For details, contact: DK Publishing Special Markets,
1745 Broadway, 20th Floor, New York, NY 10019
SpecialSales@dk.com

Printed and bound in China

The publisher would like to thank the following for their kind permission to reproduce their images:
a=above; c=center; b=below; l=left; r=right; t=top; b/g=background
Alamy Images: W. Wayne Lockwood, MD 4-5cb/g, 8-9b/g, Charles Mauzy 5tclb/g, 24-25 b/g, Craig Tuttle 4brb/g,
14-15b/g, 28-29b/g, 30acr, Phil Wilson/Stocktrek Images 16-17, Larry Lee Photography 18-19b/g, 30acl, Robert Harding
Picture Library Ltd 20-21b/g, 30ac, Jim Zuckerman 30bl; **Corbis:** Matt Brown 26-27b/g; **DK Images:** Jon Hughes 4-5c,
8-9b/g, 8b; **Getty Images:** James Randklev 4cb/g, 10-11b/g, J.P. Nacivet 22-23b/g, 30br;
Getty Images / iStock: Orla 6-7b/g, dottedhippo 9b

Cover images: *Front:* **Dorling Kindersley:** Alexandra Bye (volcano), Jenny Wren cl, br;
Back: **Dorling Kindersley:** Alexandra Bye tl, Jenny Wren cr, bl
All other images © Dorling Kindersley

For the curious
www.dk.com

Meet the
Dinosaurs

Look!
Here come
the dinosaurs.

This dinosaur
has sharp teeth.

Tyrannosaurus
[tie-RAN-oh-SORE-us]

This huge
dinosaur has
a long neck.

Brachiosaurus
[BRAK-ee-oh-SORE-us]

This dinosaur has three horns.

Triceratops
[try-SER-uh-tops]

This fast dinosaur has sharp claws.

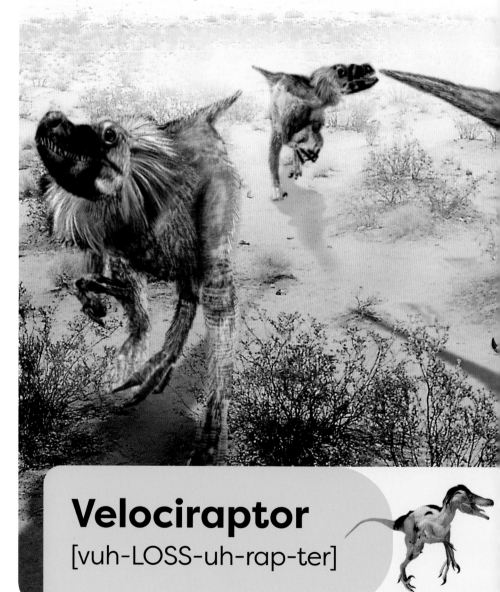

Velociraptor
[vuh-LOSS-uh-rap-ter]

Corythosaurus
[ko-RITH-oh-SORE-us]

This dinosaur has a bright crest.

This dinosaur is small.
It runs fast.

Compsognathus
[KOMP-sug-NAY-thus]

This dinosaur is smart.
It has large eyes.

Troodon
[TROH-oh-don]

This dinosaur has plates and spikes. It has a tiny brain.

Stegosaurus
[STEG-oh-SORE-us]

This dinosaur is tall.
It has thin legs
and a toothless beak.

Gallimimus
[GAL-uh-MY-mus]

Iguanodon

[ig-WAHN-oh-don]

This strong dinosaur
has a spike
on each thumb.

This dinosaur
eats plants.
It has a thick skull.

Stegoceras
[STEG-oh-CER-us]

This tough dinosaur has a tail club.

Ankylosaurus
[an-KAI-loh-SORE-us]

Which dinosaur do you like best?

Glossary

ankylosaurus
a plant-eating dinosaur with a tail club

brachiosaurus
a very tall plant-eating dinosaur

triceratops
a plant-eating dinosaur with three horns

tyrannosaurus
a large meat-eating dinosaur

velociraptor
a fast, meat-eating dinosaur with sharp claws

Ready to find out how much you learned? Read the questions and then check your answers with an adult.

1. Which dinosaur has large eyes?

2. Which dinosaur has plates on its back and spikes on its tail?

3. Which dinosaur has a bright crest on its head?

4. Which dinosaur is small?

5. Imagine if you were a dinosaur for a day. What would you eat? Would you have any special features?

1. Troodon 2. Stegosaurus 3. Corythosaurus
4. Compsognathus 5. Answers will vary